MW01230403

J. Alex Connor

BookLeaf
Publishing

India | USA | UK

Presentation by *BookLeaf Publishing*

Web: www.bookleafpub.com

E-mail: info@bookleafpub.com

ISBN: 9789358310221

First edition 2023

PREFACE

Trigger Warning:
Please note that these poems contain difficult
subject matters, such as mental illness,
self-harm, suicide, sexual harassment and
assault, and homophobia.

Doormat

If I lay beneath the floorboards,
Maybe I'll understand
why they walk all over me.

Dedication of a Mason

Brick by brick
The wall was built.
The manor's mason
Adjusted his belt
Then lay a brick
And mud another,
Squishing the next
Atop it's brother.
"This wall should soar
And touch the sky.
You're only finished
When heaven is nigh."
That was the job
The nobleman gave,
So the manor's mason
Worked himself to the grave.

Dawn's Child

The wind died down
And the crickets quit chirping
In anticipation of the dawn.
In that brief moment
Where the sun's rays
Breached the horizon
And inspected the ground
For every last shadow,
All the world's creatures knew
To hold their breath.
No bug, nor bird,
Needed to be taught this lesson;
It was innate,
But then
The bigger bodies came.
The yawning bear,
The bumbling moose,
And later,
The big bad man.
The big bodies ignored
The sacred act of light
Being laid across the land
By the roiling fire spirit
In the sky.
The bear yawned

In the morning,
Stealing dew from the air,
Into it's lungs,
Before it could be
Laser vaporized
By the sun's fiery streams.
The moose bumbled
Through the woods,
Snapping twigs and leaves
Under heavy hooves,
Forcing their held breaths
To expire
Before the sun's ritual arrival
Had passed.
The big bad man
Invented the alarm,
And, subsequently,
Became slave
To its droning.
Beep
And man wakes,
Beep
And man rises,
Beep
And man goes to work.
Before even a beam
Has blessed his face,
Man is distracted.
The sun rises,

Unnoticed
By the one,
For whom,
She created the world.

So Pretty

Dear Lord…

Please protect the bitch that calls me pretty.
If that word is uttered in my description,
let me not hear it because
I HATE the word pretty.
I DESPISE the word pretty.
Pretty is the petty cousin of Beautiful,
the lesser of the two,
the one that shows up already drunk
to the family Christmas party,
stays just long enough to flash her face,
and leaves before she remembers
how important these people are to her.
Pretty is the selfish sister of Intrigue,
the one that slut shames younger people
more colorfully clad with more exciting lives.

If you should seek to describe me
and would like to express your
appreciation of my appearance,
call me ravishing,
call me radiant,
call me glorious.

If you should seek to describe me
but my visage makes you ill,
call me sickening,
call me deadly,
tell me that you're gagging.

If you should seek to describe me
and wish to assimilate,
tell me that I'm to die for,
that I'm inspiring,
that I'm your muse.

Don't disrespect my elegance with that weak-ass
word - Pretty
Does it capture my force of personality - Pretty
Does is convey the essence of my
ever-infectious energy - Pretty

Do less, I dare you;
if pretty is the word
that hangs from your lips when you see me,
keep them shut,
because I'd rather not hear it.
There are so many more exciting words
in the dictionary,
and if it requires that you expand your lexicon,
get to work- but don't you think for a minute
that you can reduce me to pretty
with your thoughtless appeasing "compliment."

Threaten me with the bare minimum of bargain
bin words - Ha!
Say it again, and I promise, it won't be pretty.

Use(s/less)

Slice me up like deli meat,
Perhaps a capicola.
Feed me to the masses
'Til the suffering is over.
Tiny bodies' bloated bellies
Come with grim prognosis.
An out to pasture use for me
Could offer them some solace.
I've got too much hear anyway;
Been trying to shed the pounds.
Less to do with how I look,
More with how I feel.
At least I'd serve a purpose,
more than I can say for my life now.
I don't know if I'd rather be
At the whim of chaotic reality,
Or a butcher's beefing cow.

Pent Agony

A longing came screaming from its tracheal
layer
Held in the mouth cave of the damned.
It had been battering, bludgeoning the backs of
molars,
Tackled by the tongue as it ran.
Once the mouth of the cave opened,
Let out to become whole in sound
The wailing song of the wretched, of the fallen,
Was swallowed by the loneliness that did
surround.

Book of Frudd

How are your bones not powder
from the mortar and pestle process
of maintaining all those lies?
How is your blood not ichor
throbbing thick through your veins
at the toll of a heathen heart?
I wish you many forked tongue kisses
to cleanse your soul of what you harbor,
Calling it devotion,
claiming it is deliverance.
I hope that you feel the sun
upon your skeletal wings
once all the wax has melted
and all the feathers have fallen,
held aloft for a moment more,
not by act of miracle,
but to be made a mockery;
feel the sun long enough
to recognize your folly before falling.
I miss your beaming smile,
your fatherly embrace,
but remember the place from whence they came,
so step back, do I,
to observe the horror that I have beheld.
Smile into the black mirror

that shows your fingers pinning the corners
of my mouth stretched high.
I wish you the coolest slab
to rest your hot face upon
when you return from your harsh battles in the
dens.
I pray for the smallest and smoothest of stones
in abundance for your sling—
but of course you will not need them
because your giant shadow of truth
is a foe I know you would never deign to face,
not when your followers lap up your slobbering
parables
as though the dog days are all they've ever
known,
not when the truth can be constructed
from bible-paper thin prayers and wafer-strong
particle stone-
so long as they serve the purpose
of teaching the flock that its shepherd
empathizes
yet prevails on the strength of his master,
the lion most high.
Gnashing teeth and striking claws
shake the sheep
while they watch the lion
take another and another of their brethren,
but the shepherd translates for us;
"fear not, for it is his plan,

grieve not, for he takes so that he may also
give."
Be warned ye sheep of little faith
and furrowed brow and working mind,
your thoughts out loud are your death sentence
if the lion or the shepherd hears you;
"but would he, who is almighty,
be constrained to such contracts?
To pay any price at all for what he creates?
To whom does he pay?"
As the question leaves my lips,
I know, faithfully, that I am done,
for the lion sees me,
carrying in his bloodied teeth no meat of sheep,
but the sundered carcass of his own cub.

You are no shepherd you vile sinner,
you man amongst the pestilence of men,
to force yourself into the places you are not
wanted,
to paint your face with your victims' tears,
to steal the youth when you have squandered
yours.
You claim to know God you wretched beast,
but I Am God,
and my wrath and spite are boundless,
so brace yourself
to drown for an eternity
in my stalwart and just un-forgiveness.

I cast you to Hell
knowing that you cannot bear
to be looked upon with knowing eyes,
and there
all the world will be watching.

Quick To Call Her

They say she's easy,
Call her sleazy,
Truth is she just likes to fuck.
It's the only thing
She's sure she's good at,
And the only time
She's ever felt loved.

Oh Compulsion, My Captain

I pick and poke
and prod and weed
out all the roots
and corrupted seeds.
Pull out the hairs,
one strand at a time,
from this tortured
scalp of mine.
I wash and scrub
and scratch my skin
in hopes of expelling
the devils within;
the dance around
my squishy brain
leaving their footprints
to bruise and stain.
Dislodged gray matter
floats off 'til my veins
vacuum it up,
slurp it away.
It will make its way,
out to the surface
through pores and pimples
I tear at when I'm nervous.
It's my duty

to rip up my flesh,
the only illogical way
to relieve all my stress.
I confess my desire
to be rid of my skinsuit,
freed bloodied boi demon
condemned, captured in sinew.
The sores get infected.
I end up with bald spots.
Undeniably vicious circle,
these compulsions I've got.

The Shrieker

There is music
In the clouds that rain glass;
A tinkling,
shattering,
Soft sort of happiness.
Where you ask,
Could you hear
Such a symphony?
The song of the silicate,
Cottonball behemoths,
Pouring out,
Tap,
Crack,
Crash!?
Not here,
Says I, but
62 lightyears away.
You may think me foolish,
But I swear to you,
There exists such a scape,
Where wind chimes
Are rendered violent
By the nature of their making,
A place where it not only
Rains glass,

But rains glass sideways.
Wind shrieking
With such force,
Carrying the glass droplets,
With their beautiful,
Musical destructiveness.
Out there
Somewhere,
Not a child of our own sun,
Planet J62-416B
Has a song that
No mortal can survive.
No ship could land on her plains,
No currently known being
Could infect her atmosphere
Without being
Immediately
Eviscerated,
By her weather song,
Her great unheard screams.
By this truth alone,
Is it the only song
I truly ache
To hear.
I would gift her my body,
My being,
Just for a moment
Of that glorious sound.

Call Me Captain, A Haiku

I'm a ship built to
Wreck with a shit-stained poop deck.
Come my horizon!

No-Arm Bard: A Tavern Tale

There's a happy little lad
With a lute and a pan
And he plays 'em both at once,
Though he hasn't any hands.

Fiddle Dum
Twiddle Dum
toot-toot
Whee!
Please No-Arm Bard,
Play a song for me!

This happy lil lad
Lost his hands and all his fingers
But he says that he don't need 'em
Because he's a great singer.
He'll tell ya the tale
If ya tip 'em and ya linger,
Once he's performed
And had a pint; it's a zinger!

Fiddle Dum
Twiddle Dum
toot-toot
Whee!

Please No-Arm Bard,
Share your story with me!

He says I'm a wee halfling
But looks, they do deceive:
I once had ripped muscles
Swol as any arms could be.
We went on big adventures,
My party and me,
And discovered a dark dungeon
By the Cerulean Sea.
Our rogue slunk in
Quiet as he could be,
But the baddies they could smell 'em
And he let out a scream!
Without a second thought
In charges me.
Hoard of goblins that we fought-
Yes, I killed seventeen.

Fiddle Dum
Twiddle Dum
toot-toot
Whee!
Golly No-Arm Bard,
How brave ye must be!

Our wizard cast some magic
With a bit of her own flare.

The sorcerer detected
Deep below a dragon's layer.
We looted all the goblins
Before we headed there.
Then I found a chest
At the bottoms of some stairs.

Fiddle Dum
Twiddle Dum
toot-toot
Whee!
Are ya rich, No-Arm Bard,
From the treasures you thieved!?

I opened up the chest,
Reachin for the shinies in it,
But it turned out the chest
Was actually a mimic!
Sunk his teeth into me
Up to his munchin limit,
Took my beefy left arm
And seemed quite happy with it.

Fiddle Dum
Twiddle Dum
toot-toot
Whee!
Me gods! No-Arm Bard,
How bloodied was ye?

Blood was sprayin out
But thank gods for the healin
That our good ol' cleric
Was so swift at dealin.
Left the mimic to his snack,
Though nauseous I was feelin,
Continued on to the dungeon
Where we heard the dragon squealin.
The beastie sat upon his hoard,
So big he nearly touched the ceilin,
Takin pleasure in his treasure
In a manor unappealin.
Got the jump on the dragon
With the stabbies rogue was dealin.
Cast a spell with me flute
His weaknesses revealin,
Our berserker got a crit,
Max damage she was dealin,
Got the last blow with me lute
And the sent the dragon keeling!

Fiddle Dum
Twiddle Dum
toot-toot
Whee!
Oi, No-Arm Bard,
What a warrior ye be!

As we returned from depths
Of the dungeon with the dragon,
We decided to celebrate
With a meal and a flagon.
Headed for the tavern,
Threw our loot in the wagon.
Stumbled upon some bandits,
Tied us up and had us gaggin!

Fiddle Dum
Twiddle Dum
toot-toot
Whee!
No! No-Arm Bard,
lost your loot did thee?

I admit from the pre-game
Was already a bit plastered,
And thank gods 'cause the leader
Was a right sadistic bastard!
With a butcher's knife he told me,
Wasn't me gold he was after,
Started with my pinky finger,
Chopped it off with evil laughter!
Took another and another
Choppin bits off getting faster,
Til he'd carved up my right arm
Like an artisanal meats master!
We'd never have escaped

If it wasn't for our casters,
Warlock sent the bandits runnin
With a necrotic cloud gasser.

Fiddle Dum
Twiddle Dum
toot-toot
Whee!
Poor, No-Arm Bard,
Such bad luck ye had seen!

I'm lucky to be alive
Still got me friends and all my songs.
Though I loved adventurin'
I know those days are long gone.
No one ask my real name,
"No-Arm Bard" stuck real strong;
My real name is Neil,
But me pseudonym ain't wrong.
I play my lute and my pan
With magical hands I bring along,
Pay for me ale and I promise to
write ya into me next song.

Karmic 13?

It saddens me
how long I've spent
on my attempts
at what I'm not.
It mocks me
Time I can't get back
Lacking instructions
others got.
How do I know
if my heart is pure
or if I'm just luring
them into my lusty plot?
How do I determine
what's wrong or right
when the right thing
burns too hot?
Singed my hair
and fried my tongue
too many times
sipping fresh tea.
Tore at my flesh
trying to correct
all that feels wrong
with my physicality.
Repeat the words

Replay the scene
obsess
Over possible outcomes
of all the possibilities
How did we
land on that one?
Tortured and writhing
in invisible pain
but you insist I'm just trying
to hurt myself.
Wringing my hands
not because it hurts
but because
It's all I can do.
Expelling energy
in this way
keeping sweat rolling
to keep from hurting you.
Afraid not so much
of your wrath
as what it all might mean
If this is my truth.
Am I crazy,
truly gone insane?
Yes or no,
Neither comes with much proof.
I've hidden the illness
behind all the locked doors
only James P. Sullivan could access.

I tucked my voice inside a shell
now only mermaids
can reach me
and I won't be drowned
out by the masses.
Fine pretending to be interested
Pretending to desire
Until he wants to kiss me,
I lose some of my steel.
Take the kiss
with an unkind disgust
a fearful shame
a vacuous confusion.
Too naive to add it up
Not sure what variables I'm using.
Be steadfast in your
Chronic exhaustion
your ever burning
existential dread
stalwart in the improvement
of your whole self.
Stillness in the water
until the bucket descends
and somebody else
needs filled.
Give until I'm dry
long past not even a drop.
While the world works
its magic to replenish

But the issue with wells
is that people only take
and never give back where they've spent it.
Chalk it up to experience
Learning curves and
curve the grade.
Thirty years practice,
not putting myself first,
now it's myself
I've got to save.

Which is Witch

With my fingertips, I grip the glass
Of the black mirror I'm trapped behind.
As always, my reaction
is to scramble back to the other side,
to normalcy,
to certainty, slave to the routine.
Trapped here too long,
I find myself assessing where I lost myself,
slipped to this place in which,
from the rage and demons,
I cannot hide.
I hear the sounds,
look over my shoulder;
what if I accept what I am,
not what they see?
If they burn me anyway,
what does it matter whether for truth or for lie?
Delve in deeper to the dark,
leave the mirror behind to be emboldened
by the anger and passion for justice
in opposition of what they say "just" is,
or say I should accept because it "just is."
This is the season of the witch,
and she will reign with vehement power,

or in ashes, with a promise to fill and choke out
their lungs.
I have always loved the water.
Maybe in place of cleansing flame they'll drown
me after I'm hung.
I can romanticize either end,
so let's explore the embers;
I'll be strapped to the stake,
Better yet the cross,
And God will laugh as I am nailed
To the echo of his final
Mortal
Form.
I lust for an audience
To finally hear my blood curdling screams,
Here I have it
So I will shriek with the breath of all my sisters
gone before me.
My final act,
I cast one last spell
So that they may not cover their ears
Subject them to the sounds
Of all my pent up fears,
Pain and anguish of the thing,
Through their cruelty I became.
The flames lick my wounds,
Most faithful companion.
While blistering is my flesh,
Boiling is my blood.

Set free at last
In the Hell that they sent me
From the ache of my muscles
And the itch of my skin.
Then I'll haunt them,
Every one.

A Post-Op Dance With Percocet

I think I wandered
To some other where,
A place open to those
In the pitfalls of desperation.
My dreams sent me sailing
Into nightmarish memory
Of another someone else
Who must've looked much like me.
The pill that eased my pain
Also called my demons forth;
To go without and endure
Or to take and still feel poorly?
Only a limited edition,
This particular prescription,
But I see why some might seek it out.
It's exciting to be boundless,
To jump across the timelines but
There's just no way of knowing
When you'll come back down.
That's the goal, is it not?
To venture forth
But always return
To show the rest what you've found.
Sometimes the finding

Is not for the keeping.
Too dangerous to touch
Much less to hold.
Before you wake from you next adventure,
Will you have withered and grown old?
Maybe not, but your bones be brittle,
You'll feel shuddering deep in your soul.
The icy roads and cold hotels
And leering eyes and perked up ears,
The ones that chase the bullet trains
And the ones that follow to collect your fears,
They seem like characters-
Leeches more like it,
Feeding off your feeble minds
While you cower in private.
Stability isn't readily available,
It costs hours just to find the gate.
When the chills and the trembles are over,
I hope you make it home safe.

Passenger Side Paradise

My favorite streetlights are brightest
In their reflections
On rain-slick blacktop and bricks.
They offer me
A Van Gogh experience
With the proper influencers.
Placid but somehow
Still moving just beneath,
Just like my blood,
Which my body has slowed
To ensure that I am
Well saturated by their residential colors.
Celadon green and
Cerulean blue mingle
In warm, sleepy corners,
In the maroon booths
In the backseats of this club
I've stumbled into.
Under the cozy smoke layer,
The knowing and the wanting
Are all mixed together
Created a contentedness
That I've never known elsewhere.
The radio underscore
In our four-wheeled vessel

Touches my ribs and lungs,
Light fingertip taps
Of rhythm and melody
And finally
I can hear harmonies
Even if the song doesn't have one.
I am at the mercy of the sound,
Bobbing my head
Weaving my hands with the wind,
Window down,
Paint seeping in.
My golden retriever companion
Guides our boat
Down the River Brycks
And blacktop.
I hope the tires are coated
In lush oil paints
By the time we return home,
Leaving a path,
In reverse
Through this rich memory.
It would make finding my way back
Much easier, but then
I would have to grow backwards,
Forgo progress,
Abandon the new self
That took so long to nurture,
Planted in anger and heartbreak,
Watered by hammer-breaking hard labor.

Eventually, the paint coated tires
Would have spent all the colors
They'd been carrying.
The path back is no more
And I know I am better for it.
I'm grateful I gave up following the tracks,
Backpedaling to an easier naivete.
I can smile
With my feet planted firmly
In this soil,
The earth accepting me where I'm at,
My toes wiggling in the most vibrant
Pthalo green grass,
Under the comfort of cobalt skies.

Mourning Town

In Mourning Town,
The children always played in the cemetery.
Visiting any other place in the country,
The sight of kids playing
Leapfrog over tombstones might offend; not
here.
The cemetery was the only place
The children could see their families.
Outside of the hallowed grounds,
Parents and siblings became
Whispers on the wind and memories.
The cobbled stone walls seem to hold them in,
keeping them alive on the lush and manicured
grounds.

Johnathon Tobey played with his sister Addy.
She moved to the cemetery when
Tuberculosis wrapped itself to into her lungs.
She had spots of blood down the apron of her
dress
From the months she spent coughing
Before she moved away.

Michael Danbury sat with his parents
On a red-checkered picnic blanket,

Playing his finest piece of memorized music
On a small viola- Hot Cross Buns.
His parents kept their amusement discreet
When notes squeaked off key a bit,
And applauded the concert at its end.
It had taken Michael awhile
To get used to the way they looked since they
moved there;
Their burnt flesh peeling back,
Hair still aflame,
And vibrant orange sparks dancing off their
clapping hands,
But he loved them all the same.

Quarrels & Pens

The instrument of the word
is the hand
In tune with a veracious mind.
The writer may draw his pen or bow,
across cello string-lined pages,
orchestrating his declaration;
A strongly worded letter.
"You sir," the conductor begins.
Staccato blame as
the writer shells out
his quicker thoughts,
the truest emotions,
front and center.
And invigorating crescendo,
crashing symbology,
cutting metaphors,
but then, a pause.
A rest.
Realism meets truth
in gentler symphony,
lulling the reader
towards the writer's
wiser words;
"What I mean to say is..."
Rhythm and rhyme scheme

make friends
and a relaxed reader
falls in line
with the less temperamental tempo.
The reader will find
the melody quite solemn,
and the harmony
is sure to pull at
the heartstrings.
Reader and writer
make amends
by the careful song's end.
Perhaps
the writer's next song
will be better
appreciated.

Red Handed October

I was sitting there,
Bleeding out,
My feelings
Pouring from my pores.
Squeezed out like a sponge,
My mind and heart were numb.
I had my 8' by 8' box,
And the concrete jungle surround.
In the midst of millions,
The lonely had taken over.
I saw myself in the mirror;
"The needle's never been
This deep before."
It started as a blemish,
A tiny bump,
But it permeated every thought.
My fingers kept finding it.
"Stop touching your face!"
"I can't help it!
My hands are not my own."
I tore at it
Until it was open,
A birthday present,
A Christmas morning,
Just beneath my skin.
The tearing brought with it

Little to no relief,
But a rush of anxiety
With another gout of blood.
I stared at the blood sacrifice
Of my otherwise smooth complexion.
I watched the red run down my neck.
I unwittingly summoned the reaper that day.
He watched me from the corner.
He waited patiently,
In quiet,
Until I was ready to call him over.
His presence was compassionate,
Deceptively inviting was his embrace.
He took a look at my bloodied chin,
The evidence cast across the vanity.
With his long, thin fingers,
He spread the wound wide,
And began to climb inside.
I thought it was just an inspection,
But of what, I wasn't sure.
My soul had long since expired.
My hope had spoiled too.
Turning back to the mirror,
I saw him behind my eyes.
He settled beside my sclera,
Only visible now and then,
But he whispered that he would be with me
forever.
We've become unfortunate friends.

Take Me To Bed, A Haiku

A million little
Deaths make for a lifetime of
Reincarnation.

Sans Gills

I told the doctor they were gills,
He frowned and said they're not.
"Actually, they're preauricular pits,
A minor birth defect you've got."
"I swim quite well!" I did insist,
But he wasn't so amused.
Whether they were gills or cysts,
I needed them removed.

But without them now
I might start drowning.
My head is barely ever
Above the water anyway.
Comedic coincidence that so many times,
Drowning is exactly how I've described,
How it feels, for me at least,
To be alive.
Without my gills,
I wonder if a sliver of my childlike wonder,
Might have been cut out too.
I know their name now, and my "gills"
Have sucked in and tried to filter out
The scientific, medical terms,
Tainted by their unfortunate osmosis.
Is that what wears us down as we age?

Infected by perspective
We unpreparedly gain?
Our ideas shift
And ebb and flow and swim.
I think that's just the issue;
It's my mind I'm drowning in.